Past Praise

"Goodman is expert at steering our gaze to identify landmarks in the natural world to bring us safely down; these sonically rich and surprising poems are lessons in perception, obliging us to look at the world from a distance and then up close, touch what is in front of us."

—Curtis Bauer

"Henrietta Goodman's debut rivets with its accuracy, honesty and fluency. These poems have tonal ranges necessary for the complexities Goodman tackles, sometimes tames, more often allows to remain feral and wild. At times the poems read as if they were urgent instructions hell-bent on keeping us alive. *Take What You Want* isn't shy about giving us a lot of what we need."

—Dara Wier

"These well-crafted poems are reminiscent of Anne Sexton's *Transformations*; readers will look forward to witnessing the transformations to come in Goodman's future work."

—*Library Journal*

"If I think of forerunners to this collection, I am immediately reminded of Sylvia Plath's zero to the bone accuracy . . . the visceral immediacy of her poetry makes Goodman Plath's heir . . . reading and rereading *Take What You Want*, I felt as if I was being told privileged secrets as old and as necessary as the first stories and the first tellers themselves."

—*Iron Horse Literary Review*

"*Take What You Want* is all about generosity, 'including' us, via startling images and vibrant language, by involving us in the world view of a distinct speaker—daughter, mother, citizen, partner—as existence and imagination force her to ask questions, some answerable, some simply—and, in these poems, beautifully—survived."

—Christopher Davis

All That Held Us

Also by Henrietta Goodman

Hungry Moon

Take What You Want

All That Held Us

POEMS

Henrietta Goodman

Winner of the John Ciardi Prize for Poetry
Selected by Kate Daniels

BkMk Press
University of Missouri-Kansas City
www.umkc.edu/bkmk

Copyright © 2018 by Henrietta Goodman

BkMk Press
University of Missouri-Kansas City
5101 Rockhill Road
Kansas City, MO 64110
www.umkc.edu/bkmk

Executive Editor: Robert Stewart
Managing Editor: Ben Furnish
Assistant Managing Editor: Cynthia Beard

BkMk Press wishes to thank Jordan Hooper, Serena Dobson, and Rebecca Adams. Special thanks to Marie Mayhugh and Linda Rodriguez.

The John Ciardi Prize for Poetry wishes to thank Walter Bargen, Susan Cobin, Greg Field, Lindsey Martin-Bowen, Michael Nelson, Linda Rodriguez, and Maryfrances Wagner.

Financial assistance for this project has been provided by the Missouri Arts Council, a state agency. Additional support has been provided by the Miller-Mellor Foundation.

Library of Congress Cataloging-in-Publication Data

Names: Goodman, Henrietta, 1970- author.
Title: All that held us / Henrietta Goodman.
Description: Kansas City, MO : BkMk Press, University of Missouri-Kansas City, [2017]
Identifiers: LCCN 2017045555 | ISBN 9781943491124 (acid-free paper)
Classification: LCC PS3607.O568 A6 2017 | DDC 811/.6--dc23 LC record available at https://lccn.loc.gov/2017045555

ISBN 978-1-943491-12-4

Acknowledgments

Thank you to Sharma Shields at Scablands Books and Chris Murray at *Gulf Coast* for publishing the following poems:

"I think they loved each other once, or thought," "A booby trap: my father was Bluebeard," "That garnet, that mistake—a kind of force," "He showed me what he was—an altar boy,"
  Marry a Monster: Lilac City Fairy Tales, Volume 2, Scablands Books

"It wasn't innocent, the way they mocked," "Explain the what but not the why, because," "I turned my face away from where she fell,"
  Weird Sisters: Lilac City Fairy Tales, Volume 3, Scablands Books

"I called desire a lie that wants a cure," "She logged the wrongs, added her own, I guess—,"
  Gulf Coast

Thank you to the Atlantic Center for the Arts for a fellowship that allowed me to attend Patricia Smith's residency in May/June of 2014, during which I wrote much of the second section of this book. Thank you to Patricia and to my fellow associate poets Jacob Collins-Wilson, Jennifer Key, Michele Randall, Sharon Scholl, Katherine Smith, and Aliesa Zoecklein for your encouragement and companionship.

Thank you to Claire Hibbs, Romy LeClaire Loran, Amy Ratto Parks, Natalie Peeterse, and especially Karin Schalm for your wisdom, encouragement, and kindness.

Thank you to Luc Phinney for the assignments.

Thank you to BkMk Press and Kate Daniels for making this book possible.

Contents

The Opposite of Us

My mother said, *he has a nice physique*	15
Nothing to do with being chaste or loose—	16
Think of a window to a room, the space	17
I turned my face away from where she fell,	18
It wasn't innocent, the way they mocked	19
The clamor for a partner—how to give	20
Whatever broke stayed broken—the TV	21
When company could still squeeze in, my aunt	22
The emptiness she couldn't fill—that's why	23
Virga, it's called, like virgin, when the rain	24
Explain the what but not the why, because	25
They never touch, and no one touches them.	26
As though the mind's a tree that you could climb	27
Someone helpless: someone else. If he needs	28
I called desire a lie that wants a cure,	29
They spoke in archetype, and lived it, too—	30

Where She Stopped

My father said to get rid of the dogs,	33
She logged the wrongs, added her own, I guess—	34
What did it mean to her to separate	35
Almost like death, but harder to define	36
In all those lives, and these, the past never	37
I think they loved each other once, or thought	38
I was supposed to sell things too, the way	39
My mother picked the figs in August, packed	40
She knew what it was like to fall, by then,	41

That body on the floor—my grandmother,	42
So green and ever-lengthening—the grass	43
A messy awareness: my aunt kept notes.	44
To save and not to spend, and so I hid	45
A booby trap: my father was Bluebeard,	46
It would be mine, that coat she'd never worn.	47
To age, awful enough, but worse not to	48

Which Way I Flew

That night I got all Sextoned up—red lips,	51
Single, but what does single mean? Decades,	52
One absence filled, but if it's true we try	53
Beyond my reach, a way to understand	54
That garnet, that mistake—a kind of force	55
A pool game's combo shot—I watch him aim,	56
He showed me what he was—an altar boy,	57
Which way I flew? My love as pilot, night	58
No way to see the outside of the thing	59
In that magician's trick, I skewered a red	60
The single ring-necked dove, monogamous	61
My eye a stigma, narrow aperture	62
I slept then woke, most of those years a dream	63
To be, not seem—she loved the little law	64
My innocence—enough of that. And blame.	65
I packed some pictures I found in a drawer—	66

All That Held Us

The Opposite of Us

My mother said *he has a nice physique*
sometimes, about some man we didn't know.
She meant, of course, his broad shoulders, narrow
hips, the opposite of us. That antique
Southern world—not sexual, her oblique
praise, not even female. We didn't know
any men at all. I should feel sorrow
instead of blame, but even now I speak
as though she wronged me. In her white high-waist
bikini, she stood just knee-deep, the lake
a green lapping danger. She couldn't swim.
It had nothing to do with being chaste
or loose, as that was called. But what mistake
made me, and what to name it, *her* or *him*?

Nothing to do with being chaste or loose—
but loose meant what? All that held them captive,
propriety and fear—they could outlive
the men but not the body. Then, no use,
the whistles, scissors, flashlights. Who'd seduce
me, ever, the imprint of tools to drive
men off so clear on my cheek? I'd survive
that lumpy pillow, never reproduce
the impotent refusal to escape—
instilled by whom? Even the virgin birth
just ignorance of sperm and how they move.
Think of the window to a room, not rape,
for once, not rape. He's climbing in to her;
she's climbing out—do you conceive? That's love.

Think of the window to a room, the space
between her narrow thighs I used to think
meant everyone could tell—the loss like ink,
indelible. But could you just misplace
virginity? What else explains the trace
of red I rinsed from wedding sheets, the sink
that numbed my hands, or the innkeeper's wink
as he changed the damp bed? I turned my face
away. Could blood spring from the mind, and flow
from the body, a phantom hymen ripped
by force of—what? I wouldn't say desire
or grief, though grief is close. I didn't know
enough to grieve the girl I'd been. I stripped
her off, gave her away, called her liar.

I turned my face away from where she fell,
the carpet pilled with poodle fur and bleached
by Lysol and insecticide. She reached
toward my mother's shadow, stuttered a spell
no one could parse—a hex from every cell,
raging, oxygen-starved. Her daughters screeched
and raved at home, a threshold never breached
or broached in public, but people could tell,
couldn't they? My mother sang *The Old Gray
Mare*, played Old Maid—it wasn't innocent.
My aunt's friend Martha sounded like a man,
and they played Bridge. No one of us would say
the things they said across the ditch. We went
there only to return the maid, and ran.

It wasn't innocent, the way they mocked
each other, screeched and grumbled a grammar
of perfect bitterness—wore it, armor
of status, even though my mother hocked
her rings in Charlotte. So easily shocked,
my aunt had packed away the old glamour
of dances—sweat-stained dresses, the clamor
for a partner. She sprayed Lysol and locked
her door when my friends came, called me *the child*
in notes she wrote to God or no one, scraps
of paper buried under piles of stuff.
I called her *shithead* once at thirteen, wild
to separate myself, to spring the traps,
to find out whether words would be enough.

The clamor for a partner—how to give
it up? My aunt a virgin when she died,
my mother almost forty—Vegas bride,
then home again, the marriage defective,
or was she just unwilling to forgive?
Whatever broke stayed broken. If she cried,
I never saw. *Find someone to provide
for you*, she said, but what she did was live
as though no one was good enough. Mistress
of condescension, she refused to show
me how to want: idealize a man
or love his unfulfilled potential, kiss
the stupid scar that proves him no hero.
Answer when he calls your name, *Mary Anne.*

Whatever broke stayed broken—the TV
my father bought the only time he came—
at first my magic purse worked it, a game
I played for company, when company
could still squeeze in, its chain a master key
I'd shake to turn it on or off, or aim
to change the channel, little metal frame
and clasp and lime green twill, no pink for me.
She dressed me like a boy, and cut my hair
the way she'd cut her own for twenty years—
a squarish bob with bangs, almost a bowl.
Did she believe herself beyond repair,
unplugged after a flash and pop her ears
echo—not decorative or useful?

When company could still squeeze in, my aunt
had filled only the upstairs rooms—the guest
room, after hers became *a pack rat's nest,*
my mother called it, narrow paths like ants
would make from door to bed—the crazy aunt,
but no one called her crazy then. She dressed
like any teacher, sang at church. Who guessed
the emptiness she couldn't fill? You can't
know what's beyond the brick façade, the heart
that beat behind the shiny treble clef
pinned to her blouse—the house still full of years
of clothes in bags and bins, and notes she'd start
to write, and moldy bread. She'd scream us deaf
if things got moved. We learned to shut our ears.

The emptiness she couldn't fill—that's why
some girls have sex. I wore a jagged charm
around my neck, half of a heart—no harm
in letting people think some older guy
might wear the other half. I was too shy
to talk to boys I liked, too strange for them
to want to talk to me. The teenaged storm
of hormones brewed over my head, a sky
of restless wings. *Virga*, it's called, when rain
evaporates before it touches ground.
My mother called orgasm *a release
of tension*—bland and abstract, more like pain
than the second heart, the wild bird I found
in me—fluttering, mysterious pulse.

Virga, it's called, like virgin, when the rain
can't make it to the ground, but what to call
it when the ground makes of itself a wall
to block the rain, refuses to contain
the drops that pound it? If he asks, explain
the what but not the why—the door he falls
against is locked. He's not the key. It's all
you know. The body's smarter than the brain,
at least at first. So it's a gradual
deflowering—his bed, your car, the field
behind the Milestone Club—a little blood
each time, with nothing very sexual
about it. The virgin soil he unseals
in a swarm of mosquitoes turns to mud.

Explain the what but not the why, because
I can't. The woman stomping up the stairs
chants *bitch, bitch, bitch, bitch, bitch.* Her sister glares
and calls their cousins on the phone. The laws
they follow give them just the teeth and claws
of parts of speech: *bitch* is a verb she dares
to use, but not a noun. Her sister blares
complaints, and she's simply describing, jaws
clenched tight, disingenuous as I watch
from under the piano—these grammar
lessons, their private rivalry. I'm part
of it. In love or rage, they never touch.
I'm meant to judge: who's the better daughter,
the better mother, the better martyr?

They never touch, and no one touches them.
So many barricaded doors—you know
that dream in which you find a room, a glow
of lamplight, notes from a piano, dim
hum of voices? It's been there the whole time—
untapped potential of the self, as though
the mind's a tree that's drilled for sap to flow.
But what if it's the opposite for them—
the room they tiptoe toward in the dark hall
is simply closed so long it's gone, and what
if it's the body, not the mind that's shut?
So even if they tried, there'd be a wall
instead of hand or mouth. Instead of heart,
a bloodless scar, a healed, sealed cut.

As though the mind's a tree that you could climb
out of yourself—the branches of the oak
that almost touched your window, song you woke
to every morning, birds and sirens. Time
to think, when you go back, about that limb
you could have tried. Even now, would it break
or hold you? Or could you hold it? The smoke
of burning leaves drifts through the screen, the grime-
caked sill, black seam of mold below the frame.
You never knew you needed to be saved,
despite the rope tied to the bed in case
of fire, the curtains sealed against the shame
of being seen. And so the one you braved
escape for: someone helpless, someone else.

Someone helpless: someone else. If he needs
you, you're powerful. If you need him, you're
weak. You figured this much out: need was pure
survival, food and air. A cut that bleeds
needs stitches, but desire's the force that pleads
for more than life, a lie that wants a cure.
But still you didn't get it, the detour
that need could make around its source. He speeds
away and you speed after him. He calls
and says he's doing it for you, then slits
his wrists. He swallows pills and runs. He ties
a rope around a winter limb and falls,
and then it's done. And then the next one fits
his mouth around a gun and shuts his eyes.

I called desire a lie that wants a cure,
but don't assume the cure for lies is truth,
or that by cure I meant a kind of health.
In that house, moods and silence made obscure
judgments, so how could anyone be sure
what filled the gaps—willful blindness, or stealth?
They spoke in archetype—the father, youth
and age, the woods, the snake. To be mature
meant to know less, so even no and yes
became mysterious. Did my father
really send us the envelope of dimes
that rained onto the yellow carpet? Less
than a dollar's worth of scorn my mother
denies if I remind her, every time.

They spoke in archetype, and lived it, too—
the thing to do with any snake was find
a man to kill it, no matter what kind
of snake, or kind of man. They wouldn't do
that corporeal work, although they knew
exactly how it should be done. Behind
the dusty bag of Sevin where the blind
cave crickets leapt with perfect aim into
his face, he'd find the shovel they described,
and stand astride the snake, and bring the blade
down. On the concrete driveway or the ground
under the fig tree where milky sap dripped
and stung my mother's hands, the severed head
flicked out its double tongue and looked around.

Where She Stopped

My father said to get rid of the dogs,
my mother said. Was it the way she told
the story, or the way the story told?
For years, I never questioned this prologue
she wrote to our departure—first the dogs
flew to her mother's house, the ring she sold
to buy their tickets hanging like a gold
halo above their heads, and hers. She logged
the wrongs, added until they justified
their implication: leave or die. She said
he never asked what she had done, which meant
he didn't care and that she hadn't lied,
and that to him gone was the same as dead,
and so he didn't follow when we went.

She logged the wrongs, added her own, I guess—
the dog she kept alive, too weak and sick
to lift his head. I listened to music
in my room, doors locked. To choose that abyss
downstairs over the lonely, hopeless bliss
of Paul Westerberg's voice seemed sadistic:
she'd feed him with an eyedropper, he'd lick
her hand. We didn't talk about that kiss
or any other. I don't remember
how many days she begged his eyes open,
changed his bed, stroked the lumps like clustered figs
under his fur. What did it mean to her
to never share a loss? Where was I when
she picked the shovel up, began to dig?

What did it mean to her to separate
but keep his name? She called him *Daddy Lou*—
a doubleness designed to tell me who
she meant, not who he was. She didn't date;
she wore his ring, as if she could create
from his absence the kind of man she knew
he could have been, find some way to undo
him from the things that he had done, negate
all but whatever first made her say yes.
Mornings, I watched the vaguely beaming face
on the canister of Quaker Oats, his,
I thought—white hair, red cheeks, unblinking eyes
that didn't see me or anything else.
Almost like death, to sit under that gaze.

Almost like death, but harder to define
since who he would have been if he were dead
was mostly up to me. I knew he read
Macbeth, gambled in Vegas, disliked wine,
seduced my mother, tried to make her sign
his bank account into her name, she said,
to keep it safe. He liked the crust of bread
more than the crumb—his murky past, a mine
shaft that caved in as he rose out of it.
I knew three of his other children's names—
Victor, Gigi, Robert, one more. His wives
demanded maintenance, wouldn't submit
until they found him. By the time I came,
how could he find himself, in all those lives?

In all those lives, and these, the past never
makes anything from scratch, so I don't know
what secret recipe my aunt followed
to make devil's food cake for my mother
that Halloween. She let me help her stir
the batter, crack the eggs, sift the cocoa,
wrote *Happy Birthday Mary Anne* in slow
orange cursive. I think they loved each other
once, shared their mother's cookbook, watched TV.
My aunt put on the green mask, the witch hat
she wore each year to hand out candy, screech
and cackle with a terrifying glee,
and we stuck plastic ghosts, witches, and bats
into the cake, three of us, three of each.

I think they loved each other once, or thought
they did, the day they fished Lake Elsinore
from a sailboat he'd bought—a whim before
they conceived me. But for years, when I thought
of them, I saw her as myself. She taught
me high waves, empty sky and distant shore,
his pride and disregard that grew the more
she panicked. I don't know whether they caught
any fish, whether he was competent
or reckless, savior or endangerer
or both, two men in one. He pulled the brim
of his hat down, opened a beer. It meant
that he had put her here and he could steer
or not steer. I was supposed to love him.

I was supposed to sell things too, the way
my father did. I'd advertise, and learn
how commerce worked—from lemonade, I'd earn
the net. My mother said the cost should stay
in the kitty, which meant I had to pay
for cups and lemons, sugar. The return
was less and more than usual. I turned
into a girl who understood that play
came last—reward, dessert—and that I worked
for her, resourcefulness my only chore.
I pulled wild onions from the neighbors' lawn
and peddled weeping figs my mother picked.
Where did she put the coins she asked me for—
petty cash, sticky from my hands, then gone?

My mother picked the figs in August, packed
them into pints and quarts and sent me out
to pull my wagon door to door, devout
and terrified—her need to sell abstract,
mine based in pure obedience, a fact.
It didn't matter what I sold—Girl Scout
cookies, toboggan hats. I want to doubt
she knew what it was like, how I backtracked
and stalled, then plodded on. I couldn't skip
even a vacant house, or the blue door
the same old woman always slammed, the man
who asked me in. In the drive-thru, I'd slip
from car to car. I sold, she watched. Unsure,
both of us, where she stopped and I began.

She knew what it was like to fall, by then,
to be that body on the floor, that mouth
leaking wet syllables, a tattered moth
among the butterflies, to be a *been*,
past tense. And so a limbo, one RN
per shift, grumpy, impatient—Granny's bath
a sponge and pan, her meals a yellow froth
poured through a tube. The summer I was ten,
the car broke down, and so we walked each day
to supervise the aides, my mother's back
a brick-red sheet I peeled twice before
it browned into filial piety—
a naked spectacle of time's attack
on flesh, and for each one of us, no cure.

That body on the floor—my grandmother,
whom I remember mostly as a hole
in memory, a vacant lap, my sole
impression from ten years a distant blur.
She kept a kind of peace, I think—a fear-
induced truce, so her daughters played the roles
she wrote—pretend, pretend, pretend, control
themselves. Something was wrong with them, and her,
and me. She taught me to crochet one strand
of olive yarn—the slip knot, then the chain
stitch, green and ever-lengthening but not
attached—an endless setting out for land
unknown, no rows, no circling back—the skein
unraveling as I went, but never cut.

So green and ever-lengthening—the grass
required a man to cut it once a week,
the pipes required a man to fix the leak,
the car required a man to pump the gas
for it. But these weren't men my mother's class
could see. These were bodies for hire. She'd sneak
a glance as her own body birthed a bleak,
messy awareness, dripped and yawned. Trespass
was no crime if you let him in, no sin
without belief. Dwayne didn't have a job.
He rode a skateboard, stole from the Quik Stop:
roses and cigarettes, a felt-tip pen,
and sketched a garden on my skin from knob
of clavicle to breast, stomach, and hip.

A messy awareness: my aunt kept notes.
Tucked in among the other mysteries—
a wedding band, a Stetson hat—a grease-
stained scrap of envelope scribbled with quotes
that showed how she'd been used—not anecdotes,
just fragments she had dreamed or heard, not keys
to any code. And then the claim she'd squeezed
along the gummy edge, stuck with dust motes—
Mary Anne tried to kill herself. Fourteen
and bored, I pillaged the crisp stacks of germ-
free bills my aunt requested at the till
and then forgot. But this I'd never seen.
To save, and not to spend—who could confirm
it real or counterfeit, worth all or nil?

To save and not to spend, and so I hid
them in my jewelry box, these truths or lies—
delusions, possibly, but whose? The prize,
a booby trap, a sting. I closed the lid.
Every claim prefaced by *she said*, so did
he hit her, or did each of them revise
themselves to victim, let spite colonize
their rendering? I still can't close the lid,
but *Mum's the word*, my mother said. She meant
the small white tin of thick rose-scented cream
she rubbed under her arms. She'd lost her sense
of smell, and so she'd ask: *deodorant?*
I sniffed, but she was odorless each time.
Of course I had no answers, then or since.

A booby trap: my father was Bluebeard,
though not a murderer. But how they killed
part of themselves to get away was still
a kind of violence. They disappeared,
his wives, but was this what he sought, or feared?
And who my mother turned into—the thrill
of his life spilling into hers—it filled
her, changed her, then she poured it out, the shared
undrinkable cocktail of their future
flushed. So, for all of us, a loss. She kept
a coat he gave her—the crushed velvet pelt
of fetal lamb, or lambs—patchwork suture
of black to white that loosened as it slept.
It would be mine, that coat, that shame I felt.

It would be mine, that coat she'd never worn.
I petted it. The glossy swirls of wool
had yellowed, like old teeth. To age, awful
enough, but worse to age like this—unborn,
a fleece first drenched in blood, then rinsed, not shorn
but skinned. Like all his gifts, impractical,
extravagant: for me, at four, a pearl
necklace. For him, easier to adorn
than love. And so the coat—a golden fleece.
And so the necklace broke; the pearls rolled, lost.
If guilt's the opposite of innocence,
then what's experience? And what release
in silence or in song? We learn the cost
and pay it, whether for greed or penance.

To age, awful enough, but worse not to
resist. When I was five, she did one thing
without me: she took off her wedding ring,
put on a dress her mother bought, a new
pair of heels. Or maybe the same flat shoes
she always wore, and maybe, too, the ring,
the undershirt. I might remember wrong,
or I made that mother up—swirls of blue
and green across the flared ivory skirt,
the sleeveless top. Twenty-five years before,
most likely to succeed. Why go, if not
to prove she did—to see who's fat, to flirt
with restless men? Why go single and poor,
if not to be the girl that time forgot?

Which Way I Flew

That night I got all Sextoned up—red lips,
a vintage polka-dotted dress, rhinestone
earrings. Single at forty-three, I'd grown
volition, finally, and learned to sip
a drink, and when I stood, hand on my hip,
to read these poems behind the microphone,
a man in the back row whispered "she's *fine*,"
and it was true—this dress mine to unzip
or not, this story too. An older man
asked later if I'd ever tried to write
something positive about my father
and while I wondered if he meant *certain*
or *nice*, he asked didn't I think it might
be therapeutic. So this, my answer.

Single, but what does single mean? Decades,
she thought someone would tell her when she changed
from wife to widow, but who would? Estranged
but not divorced, oblivious, she stayed
true by default. He'd be in some arcade
in Vegas, broke or flush, third wife exchanged
for fourth. I used to think I could arrange
a kind of coup—whatever game he played,
I'd hold him at gunpoint until he won
enough for me to get the boy I loved
out of Gastonia before he killed
himself. Under the California sun,
we'd change our names, eat oranges, live above
a store, the two of us one absence, filled.

One absence filled, but if it's true we try
to replicate, not remedy, the lack,
then that first boy, his thumbnails painted black,
his hair liberty spiked and streaked with dye—
a copy, not a prototype. He'd die
beyond my reach, the way he lived—soundtrack
of his own losses a loop of feedback
I couldn't interrupt, a lullaby.
And yet I have the ordinary list
he sent—the yellowed envelope, his hand.
Why he loved me: I wore fishnets, sang well
(which wasn't true), I smiled, I liked the Smiths,
my mother cooked weird food, I drove a van,
had a blind dog, didn't believe in hell.

Beyond my reach, a way to understand
the mind that thinks, *if you like silver, make
him buy you platinum, or white gold.* Don't take
his word to signify your worth—your hand
requires a sign the world can see. Demand
a signifier you can pawn, no fake
diamond, or worse, that garnet, that mistake,
a crude little flame like the ones you panned
for in the creek with the Girl Scouts. The ring's
your alimony. Or, the ring's a seed,
an aril like the ones Persephone
swallowed in hell—that chthonic fruit, a spring
that streams both birth and death, a rock that bleeds,
and signifies: nothing, no one is free.

That garnet, that mistake—a kind of force
equal and opposite the one you made
before, a pool game's combo shot. You played
to test the laws of motion—less excuse
this time—you knew better, tried to seduce
yourself. His beauty helped, and so you weighed
the options, waited for your doubts to fade,
conceived his child, put on his ring. Of course
you were afraid of loneliness. You hung
new photos, labyrinth in every frame.
He looked like James Dean, shivered when you'd trace
the soft blade of his hipbone with your tongue.
And you thought that would be enough—the same
maze built too well again, the same walled place.

A pool game's combo shot—I watch him aim,
draw back the stick and pause to roll his sleeves,
then sink the ball and run the rest. He leaves
at two a.m., and I'm with him—his game
a brief but absolute attention, claim
and drift, so long ago and still—retrieve
and squander. Years of that betrayal. Why grieve?
He showed me what he was, a bull not tame,
just led by pain, or fear of pain. He pierced
the center of his nose and wore a ring,
a paradox: he might follow, but what
would lead except his own half-drunk and fierce
and stubborn hand, and where would that hand bring
him but right back to the same door he shut.

He showed me what he was—an altar boy,
a drunk, a tragic hero, fingers stained
from nicotine. His posture—force restrained,
potential, not kinetic. He'd destroy
then resurrect himself, transformed by joy—
a passing radiance in darkness. Trained
to find the fatal flaw, I read his feigned
achievements, paralytic fear: alloy
of character and man. *Which way I fly
is Hell; myself am Hell*—Satan, my twelfth
grade English crush—and so I analyzed
the text and not the reader, not the why
of my pursuit of ruined beauty, wealth
of loss, not what, in me, he recognized.

Which way I flew? My love as pilot, night
in spring, the plane small as a car. My sons
asleep in the back seat, our town's beacon
revolving on the mountain, blinking white
and red. An aureole around each light,
like caterpillar webs in trees or spun
sugar or baby's breath. I loved no one
in that sweet haze, no one not on that flight,
our self-contained, transparent globe propelled
by thrust and trust. Each time, no way to see
the outside from the inside, so instead
I'd watch the shadow of the plane that held
us rise along the narrow strip as we
came down to meet it on that field, that bed.

No way to see the outside of the thing
that holds you in—the plane, the house, the life.
Of all the ways to pierce the body—knife
or needle—still, the self's a fairy ring,
mysterious, contained. And when two rings
are linked in that magician's trick called Wife
and Husband, more the mystery, their grief
and private joy. But in our case, the rings
were forged of logic, a Venn diagram,
the intersection of two sets—the third
an accident, an almond, alien
and liminal, a grain of rice, a lamb.
Not mine or yours, I thought, when I first heard
his cry and touched the softest fleece, his skin.

In that magician's trick, I skewered a red
balloon like a kabob—the needle sheathed
in Vaseline. No pop. The skin just breathed
a little sigh and let it through. I fed
the single ring-necked dove, sold wigs to rude
clowns, dusted the black canopy of teeth
that hung above the rack: Table of Death,
no hoax in that predicament. I'd spread
my arms and legs under the real threat
of imminent impalement, shackled tight,
the man-sized hourglass draining fast. I'd play
the damsel in distress, my legs fishnet,
mascara smeared, then save myself—not flight
or fight or freeze, but escapology.

The single ring-necked dove, monogamous
or abstinent—collared and caged, tethered
as ever to the cote and hand, less bird
than kite. My first trip home, I rode a bus
three days—Missoula, Minneapolis,
Chicago, Charlotte—cities gray and blurred
in January rain. The moans I heard
just pigeons in the eaves, a bored chorus,
Gregorian and local as I'd be
if I had stayed—a needle in a drawer,
my eye a stigma, little empty slit,
my tip a sharp but idle anther, he
or she or neither. I'd lie still, ignore
the buzz and coo and thrust, immaculate.

My eye a stigma, narrow aperture
or bulb—receptacle through which the grains
of pollen pass. A body with no brain
but bloom—I never was that perfect, pure
autoerotic flower, never sure
of anything that entered—was it pain
or bliss that longing brought, and would it wane,
or when? And why was certainty both lure
and bore? I mistook fear for love again,
then mistook love for fear and almost lost
my own and his. No fairy tale but this:
I waited naked on a white wolf skin—
my camouflage, the guard hairs tipped with frost.
I slept then woke, opened my eyes, said yes.

I slept then woke, most of those years a dream
not worth remembering. Afraid of men,
obedient, unblemished, I was ten
but swam in a placental dusk, a seam
of light around a door. *To be, not seem*—
the motto of our state, but what I'd been
I didn't understand—stripped to bare skin,
my feet in clamps—condensed into a scream
that filled the waiting room—*Ms.* magazine
and *Let It Be*. My mother listened, flipped
the pages, tapped her foot. The steel table
I lay on knocked against the wall between
us as she sat where she was told and lapped
a cup of coffee—still inscrutable.

To be, not seem—she loved the little law
of adage, the façade without the mess
of motive. Wait for him to ask, say yes,
be nice—you're lucky if he wants to paw
your pimpled skin or let his tongue, that raw
wet oyster, occupy your mouth. Your dress
is paper, made to tear. To acquiesce
is woman—close your eyes, unhinge your jaw—
it's fast, and faster if you don't resist.
Girls put things in their bodies and then lie,
the doctor said, and what he put in me
I still don't know. And when I tried to twist
away, he held me down, his alibi
my innocence, my mother's pedigree.

My innocence—enough of that. And blame.
Either she hid too much, or not enough.
A kind of double jeopardy—the snuff
tin printed with a golden peach, my shame
at being fooled. No wonder beauty's claim
seemed false, not worth the price. She called its bluff,
refused it. So we're back to this—the stuff
my aunt ordered from L.L.Bean still came
for weeks after she died—shirts that repelled
mosquitoes, huge flashlights. My mother stacked
them in the hall—above our heads, this last
layer of a life unlived. The house still smelled
of bug spray and banana peels. I packed
some pictures and some makeup, left the rest.

I packed some pictures I found in a drawer—
my bare-armed mother on an evening pier:
earrings like tusks, a shiny dress, her hair
cut short. She gazes toward the sea or shore,
unlike the way my father in his store
stares straight ahead, his almost-smile clear
against a blurred backdrop of skis, hardware,
guitars and fishing rods. And then one more
of him with me—a baby whispering
a secret in his ear, my fingers pressed
over his lips. They loved each other once,
and here is proof. In each, the one taking
the picture's left behind, shadow or less,
but look at all that's there, shaped by absence.

Henrietta Goodman is the author of two previous books: *Hungry Moon* (Mountain West Poetry Series) and *Take What You Wan*t (Beatrice Hawley Award, Alice James Books). Her poems have appeared in *Gulf Coast*, *Field*, *New England Review*, and other journals. She has attended the Marjorie Davis Boyden Wilderness Writing Residency, as well as residencies at the Atlantic Center for the Arts and the Kimmel Harding Nelson Center. Originally from North Carolina, she lives in Missoula, Montana.

This book is set in Appareo, Helvetica and Garamond.

Winners of the John Ciardi Prize for Poetry

The Resurrection Machine by Steve Gehrke, selected by Miller Williams

Kentucky Swami by Tim Skeen, selected by Michael Burns

Escape Artist by Terry Blackhawk, selected by Molly Peacock

Fence Line by Curtis Bauer, selected by Christopher Buckley

The Portable Famine by Rane Arroyo, selected by Robin Becker

Wayne's College of Beauty by David Swanger selected by Colleen J. McElroy

Airs & Voices by Paula Bonnell, selected by Mark Jarman

Black Tupelo Country by Doug Ramspeck, selected by Leslie Adrienne Miller

Tongue of War by Tony Barnstone, selected by B. H. Fairchild

Mapmaking by Megan Harlan, selected by Sidney Wade

Secret Wounds by Richard Berlin, selected by Gary Young

Axis Mundi by Karen Holmberg, selected by Lorna Dee Cervantes

Beauty Mark by Suzanne Cleary, selected by Kevin Prufer

Border States by Jane Hoogestraat, selected by Luis J. Rodríguez

One Blackbird at a Time by Wendy Barker, selected by Alice Friman

The Red Hijab by Bonnie Bolling, selected by H. L. Hix

All That Held Us by Henrietta Goodman, selected by Kate Daniels